Pippi Rocks

More Stories from the Dog Blog

Author: Pippi Babson

Dictated to: Katherine L. Babson, Jr.

Illustrated by: Katherine K. Macdonald

Cover and Book Design: Katherine K. Macdonald

1

Pippi Rocks, More Stories from the Dog Blog

Facebook Blog @ Katherine Babson
Text © Katherine L. Babson, Jr.

Illustrations © Katherine K. Macdonald,
TheRedHorseGallery.com

Editor: Katherine L. Babson, Jr.

Book Design/Art Direction: Katherine K. Macdonald

First printed 2023

Books by Pippi:
Tails with Gig, Stories from the Dog Blog; Available at WellesleyBooks.com and Amazon.com, 2022
Pippi Rocks, More Stories from the Dog Blog; Available at WellesleyBooks.com and Amazon.com, 2023

Dedication

To all those veterinarians
who take such good care of dogs
and
who love them so very much.

Foreword

It has been a year of ups and downs for me. I've been a best-selling author, which I have adored, taken on numerous internships, and done some mentoring—sometimes successfully and other times not. I've been through and recovered from a very nasty illness. And, almost too often to mention, I have been caught red-handed with purloined goodies from the kitchen. That's a lot for a Young Dog.

My favorite thing, though, is walking and hiking with my owner, Katherine (Gig) Babson. One of our favorite places is Dogtown, an abandoned settlement located in the middle of Cape Ann, Massachusetts, where you can see the Babson Boulders, 26 big rocks engraved with inscriptions such as Kindness; Help Mother; Courage; Work; Never Try, Never Win; and others. One of Gig's relatives (which makes him my relative, too), Roger Babson, hired unemployed stonecutters from the Cape's granite quarries during the Great Depression to carve the boulders. Roger Babson also founded Babson College, but you won't find any of the boulders there. That's okay—the students are too busy with their studies to be looking in the woods for rocks.

Dogtown is where I learned the command "Boulder!" I jump up on one of the big rocks, sit and stay, and then get a yummy treat. Gig believes in that fancy word "osmosis" and thinks that the sentiments on the rocks will somehow rub off on me. She is particularly interested in "Help Mother" and "Kindness."

I call the boulders my Pippi Rocks. Most of the stories in this book (many of which first appeared in my dog blog) illustrate them. My goal is to live up to their lofty sentiments.

I hope you think I do.

Love,
Pippi

Dogtown

Dishwashing

My boyfriend, Moose, told me about Mother's Day the other day on our walk. Since I was just a puppy last year, he said, Gig had had no expectations from me, but this year would be different. In his house, they celebrate with a special meal. His family are all good cooks, and Moose is responsible for cleanup—his dream job. He loves it! I know I would like it, too, but Moose cautioned me to avoid doing anything that might bring up bad memories.

Drats. That considerably narrows my options. I can't do cleanup because I was caught sitting in the dishwasher when I was a puppy. I can't suggest my favorite meal, a stuffed roast chicken, after I once ate the whole chicken, including the stuffing and vegetables, and left no trace of it. And there was the time I knocked a pan of those scrumptious blueberry muffins to the floor and gobbled up the muffins and their paper wrappers.

Grilling a nice piece of salmon or a juicy steak is also out, because I pulled the drippings pan from under the grill last fall. What a mess that was! I knocked over the grill and took the tray to the side yard, where I lapped up the drippings and tore the tray to shreds, to the neighbors' delight and Gig's mortification.

At the moment, unless someone has a better idea, I may suggest to Gig that she and I have quality time together making peanut butter pumpkin dog biscuits in heart shapes to show that I love her.

Leaf Jumping

It was Thanksgiving weekend. I had planned to help Gig rake leaves, which, honestly, seems such a silly thing to do. We enjoy leaves up in the trees for months and we watch them as they change to the most magnificent colors and then start falling off and floating to the ground. Next comes the chore of raking them up. I don't know for certain, but it seems folks are cranky when they rake leaves. I know I get cranky. I can't stand the ear-piercing noise from those snakelike gadgets that swallow the leaves.

I decided rather than rake leaves, why not take Gig on a walk to find the perfect leaf pile? I am sure you are asking yourself, "How hard can that be in late fall in New England?" Well, I can tell you: It is very hard. Almost all the perfect piles are in someone else's yard.

Eventually, we found a perfect mountain of leaves blocking a sidewalk and spreading out into the street. I hopped up on the brick wall next to the pile and pranced down to the end. I heard "Jump!" and I flew into the air and landed in a belly flop right in the middle of that glorious pile! I used my dog paddle, perfected over the summer, to swim back to the top of the pile. What joy! I did it over and over again.

Most of my thanks this weekend are reserved for my family, friends, and fans. I hope yours are, too!

Unwinding

Today is my Gotcha Day, the two-year anniversary of the day Gig took me from my birth mother. I had been looking forward to celebrating the day with her. I thought we might enjoy a take-out dinner from the local pet store. I had noticed some fresh-meat options in the big fridge there that would make a very special meal for me. I sense it is not going to happen, though. Well, I am sure of it now, because it is almost dinnertime.

It's all due to those New Year's resolutions that I was coerced into signing last month. One of them is "Eschew chewing all leather products." For starters, "eschew" is rather a big word for a Young Dog like me, but I figured it out. I had thrown it on the list because I figured the opportunities for mishaps were slight. How wrong I was!

I was sitting next to Gig while she was completely immersed in a phone conversation with a classmate about why it is always a good thing to support one's alma mater. She was wearing her new wool sweater, which, honestly, she has worn every day since Christmas. It was only "up close and personal," as they say, that I noticed a little square on the sleeve.

I waited until she took the sweater off and tossed it on the floor, like she does with all her clothes. I started to investigate that sweater. Maybe that little square was dirt or a piece of food stuck on the sweater. Gig is a messy cook, after all. It turned out to be a most tasty piece of leather! I chewed it off the sweater and then tugged at the yarn. It just kept unwinding. What fun!

She didn't even notice. Well, of course she did notice, but it was much later in the day.

No special treats that day!

Flying Ace

Here's the question of the day: Who should know you better—your owner or your owner's friends? The obvious answer is your owner—the one who spends most of every day with you. But not in my case.

We ended our summer with a relaxing couple of days on a Cape Cod beach. Our host was a member of our Pandemic Pod, made up of three humans and three dogs. I was the only four-legged one who made the cut for the trip to the beach. We had the very best time. I swam in the ocean, walked for miles along it, and rolled in the sand. It was heaven!

I did not want to spend one minute away from my Pod friends. Apparently, they did not feel the same way about me, because, for some reason known only to them, they actually wanted to take a walk without me. The host suggested I stay inside the house, but Gig said, "Oh, no, don't worry. She knows how to stay." So they deferred to Gig and left me on the gorgeous porch, which has wide windows overlooking a very long hill down to the beach.

Forget the "stay"! I could not stand it for one minute. I jumped! Oh, I soared through the air like Snoopy the Flying Ace. What fun! What freedom! I thought maybe I could be a pilot. And then I landed. You might describe it as a crash landing—a major one at that. It took my breath away!

I got up, trotted down to the beach, took a swim, and sunned myself. My Pod friends looked at Gig and said, "Told you so!" Those friends knew me better than Gig does.

What does that say about our relationship?

Dog Paddle

When you are a Young Dog, all sorts of internships pop up. Take yesterday, for example. I agreed to an internship as a paddleboard coach. It came up so quickly that I didn't even have time to watch a video on training techniques. The head coach told me I was going to have a challenging student—someone old and a bit uncoordinated. I said, Bring it on! And, then I found out that my student was Gig!

As you can see, I coached her to paddle from a kneeling position. I knew then that I should have insisted that she stick with her yoga classes.

To stand up, first one foot down, then the other, end in a crouching position, take a deep breath, and up you go. Was she wobbly or what? She seemed not to understand the "take a deep breath" part, but after I swam many times around the board, encouraging her with sharp barks, she did it!!

We got back to the dock and, of course, Gig bragged to everyone that she had been paddleboarding all around the cove, when, of course, she barely got up.

I was physically and emotionally exhausted from the ordeal and took a long nap. When I woke up, I checked to see about dinner. Three delicious hamburger patties were sitting on the counter, ready for grilling. But wait! No vegetarians among the four of us—the head coach, Gig, her brother, and me—so someone was going to be left out. Just in case I was the one, I quickly gobbled up two of the patties. I left one on the plate on the misguided theory that the others would not argue over it and would just give it to me.

Wrong again—no arguments and no third burger for me.

Ronan—Get Wet!

I am not entirely sure I have potential as a coach in water sports. I have now worked with two challenging students. One, of course, was Gig. Even though the water was as smooth as a mirror, it took some clever coaching to get her up on the paddleboard.

The other student did not like to swim. I was asked if I might help my friend Ronan, a 175-pound Newfoundland dog who is my age, to get up the courage to swim. Newfies are great water dogs, and his sister is a certified water-rescue dog, but not Ronan. As you can see, he has to wear a life preserver.

My job was to walk into the pond with Ronan and get him swimming. Really, how hard could that be?? Well, it was. Only a few steps in, I was swimming while Ronan could still walk with his feet planted firmly on the sandy bottom. I stayed next to him and encouraged him to walk deeper into the pond. Pretty soon the ground left Ronan, and he was dog-paddling. Shocked that he was waterborne, he immediately turned and aimed for shore. I gently nudged him to keep it up.

He went maybe 10 feet before he regained the sandy bottom, and that was it. He bolted for shore and just stood there in his life preserver. He was praised for being so brave and was given some very tasty treats.

Really, how does that work? He was rewarded with the best treats I have seen in months, and for what? Wearing a life preserver and dog-paddling for a few strokes. What did I get? "Thanks for trying, Pippi."

How fair is that?

Hitched

I now have five mountain ascents under my collar. I have been basking in compliments from other hikers: "Oh, she is so cute!" "She was very respectful and did not bother me when she went by me." I come every time I am called, and I wait for Gig to catch up.

It was simply time to change the narrative. I was bored with waiting for Gig. She is very slow. When two men passed us yesterday on a mountain trail, I could smell some pretty interesting food in their packs. I ignored Gig's calls to "Come!" and just trotted right behind them. I left Gig way down the mountain.

What do you suppose happened? They tied me to a trail sign and said, "Stay." They found Gig's cell phone number embroidered on my handsome red collar, called her, and told her where to find me. They left me all by myself. Just like that. No food, no water, no Gig. I mustered up my courage and waited. What else could I do?

You can guess who hustled up that mountain at triple speed. And you can guess who now makes me recite Mountain Protocol—stay together, never leave someone alone—as if it was a prayer.

I get it. I better stick with Gig, the slowpoke.

My First 4,000-Footer

I did it! I hiked my first 4,000-foot peak in New Hampshire yesterday. Hooray for me!

It was a whole day of "Good, Pippi." "Nice job, Pippi." I didn't follow any strangers; I waited for Gig and her friend to catch up to me. Sometimes I went ahead to scout out stream crossings and boulder fields, but I always came back when called. Not one reprimand the whole day. A record. Imagine that.

To be completely honest, there was one minor incident. At our lunch stop, I showed off. We went through my entire trick routine for her friend, except the pick-my- pocket trick. Then I remembered it! While no one was looking, I picked the pocket of her friend's backpack and found a discarded sandwich wrapper. I grabbed it. Nothing was in it, but I shredded it anyway. That was it. Nothing more than that.

New Hampshire has 48 peaks over 4,000 feet, and yesterday's, Mount Moosilauke, is the 10th highest of them all. Gig says I have plenty of courage and am such a good hiker that I could earn my 4,000-Foot-Peak Bagger Badge for Canines. But she says that unfortunately she's too old now to do them all again, and she doesn't want me to do them alone. That's okay. I would rather just hike with Gig wherever she takes me.

I am growing up a bit, don't you think?

Bouldering

Have you ever been asked to mentor someone, to guide them in their personal development? It is quite remarkable that, even as a Young Dog, I have been entrusted to mentor someone—well, someone's dog.

The dog in question is Clara, my illustrator's dog. She is an Airedale and at age 6 months she weighed more than I do now. In other words, she is a very big dog—at least that is how she seems to me.

In anticipation of Clara's upcoming American Kennel Club Trick Test, I endeavored to show her a new trick: how to "boulder." That is the simple command for a dog to jump up on a big rock, sit, and stay. If successful, the dog gets a treat. I showed Clara how to do it.

Clara was so eager to get that treat that she jumped up on the rock on top of me, pushed me to the side, and knocked me off the rock.

Clara got the treat, of course!

I said, "That's it. I quit."

Author's Roadshow

As many of my fans know, last year I published my first book, *Tails with Gig*. Here I am being congratulated by my close friend Peter, who is the manager of our local bookstore, for being the author of the best-selling book during the holiday season.

Being an author is hard work. It takes a lot more than dictation to Gig, let me tell you. You have to have the "material," which in my case is not difficult. Just look at what's been done with it: There's the piece in the *Boston Globe* (the Sunday edition, no less); or the story in Babson College's entrepreneurship blog, "Puppy Unleashes Lessons in Publishing"; or one of my favorites, the item in our town blog, "Wellesley Black Lab pup becomes a local literary sensation."

Even the town library got into the act. My book was the subject of one of the floral arrangements for "Books in Bloom," the library's big fundraiser. It featured the story of my grabbing the open tuna fish can and running off with it to the back yard. (I haven't had any tuna fish since then, but I still remember how good it was.)

Then there are the paw signings, the photo ops, the business cards, and even the baseball cards.

The demands on an author are endless.

Party Favors

For my paw signings, Gig and my illustrator, Kathy Mac, planned to put together goody bags filled with my signature pumpkin peanut butter dog biscuits. Kathy's dog, Clara, came over to help. They set up shop on our dining room table.

I am supposed to mentor Clara, so I thought it might be a good time to teach her how to take food off a dining room table. I got up on my hind legs and showed her how to pull the tablecloth to the edge of the table and then swat at the biscuits to bring them closer to us.

While Clara watched, I was able with some effort to get several dog biscuits to the edge of the table, intending to share them with her. What did Clara do? She's so big, she simply put her head on the table and ate every one of them. Not one crumb for me.

I took Kathy aside and said that Clara was an impossible student and needed to go to a canine school for problem dogs.

Paw Signings

Sometimes you start something and don't know where it will lead. Has that ever happened to you?

Being an author is a good example. Would you believe that once you've written a book, you might have to sit under a table for hours? That's a book signing for you, although it's a paw signing in my case. Gig and my illustrator, Kathy, sit at the table and sign my name and then stamp my paw print on the books.

And what about me? It's not very different from every other day in my life when I look up and just see pants, skirts, socks, shoes and sometimes toes. Believe me, they look the same from under the table.

I try to pass the time under the table by making a game out of it—I sniff and can tell which legs belong to a person who owns one of my kind. I can tell who might—heaven forbid—own a cat.

Once in a while I am surprised to see something down by an ankle, like a drawing. I licked one once to see if it might be food that splashed on the leg, but it seemed to be permanent.

And toes? I can go on for a long time about toes. Maybe I should try nail polish on mine. Red would work—it would go with my red collar and signature red scarf.

A Reading

I did my first reading this week in the library of an elementary school, for two separate groups of first-through-third-graders. I loved it. The kids were great!

If you are not an author, you might not know that authors are expected to read from their books at gatherings in bookstores, libraries, schools, and other venues. Because I can't read out loud, I enlisted Gig as my assistant for the day. Gig and I got all dressed up. I made sure that my signature red scarf was laundered and ironed. For Gig, as you know by now, it was much more of an ordeal, but somehow she managed to look the part.

On our way to the school, I selected the stories from *Tails with Gig* that I wanted her to read. Our first session went very well. She stuck to the script and read from my book. The kids were attentive, and they seemed to like the stories. At the end of the class, they lined up to pet me. I wagged my tail extra hard for the ones who had treats for me.

But the second group? No doubt you think I was the one to act up. You're wrong—it wasn't me. It was Gig. She decided to act out my stories! There's "Fishy Business," about when I stole the opened tuna-fish can off the counter, took it out to the yard, and devoured the contents. In the story, Gig corners me in the yard and says, "Let me smell your breath." In the class, she actually got on her hands and knees and bent right down in my face and said, "Let me smell your breath," just like the story! The kids all laughed, but I didn't. I take this author business very seriously.

I am lining up other reading engagements now. You can reach me here or on my very own Facebook page, Tails with Gig, which I have just made public, and we can schedule a time. I have to read locally, though, because my driver is unreliable!

Ball Dog

We were watching the U.S. Open Tennis Championships earlier this fall. I loved watching it and thought,"I could be an excellent ball dog, chasing after all those tennis balls." Sure enough, an opportunity presented itself. Just like that. And as I have always said, *Carpe diem*.

It was a family barbecue. While the cooks were preparing the meal, Gig's brother, Bub, and his granddaughter engaged in a little lacrosse practice. It appeared to be an odd pairing, if you ask me. Bub is old (older than Gig, which means he is *old*). He played lacrosse in the previous century and coached and refereed at college lacrosse games. He seemed a bit rusty to me. His granddaughter is on a middle school team and actually plays the game.

That ball was in the woods, under the grill, across the lawn, and occasionally landed in one of those funny little baskets at the end of the sticks. Back and forth, around and about, I chased after that lacrosse ball and each time brought it back and dropped it at the feet of one of them. Actually, it was exhausting.

And what do you suppose? At suppertime, while they feasted on chicken and all the trimmings, I ate my lonely bowl of dry kibble and listened to them talk about me. Bub told them how surprised he was—that he had been sure I would run off with the lacrosse ball, perhaps chew it, and surely would cover it with my spit. Instead, I retrieved the ball and returned it unharmed—and, best of all, not covered with slime.

I guess Bub thinks of me as a simple little Lab and forgets that my full title is Labrador *Retriever*. Of course I fetch and return. It is as simple as that.

I wish everything were so simple, don't you?

Being Sick

Have you ever been sick? I mean, *really* sick? I was. I hurt all over and had headaches. I wondered whether I'd ever play again with my dog pals or chew my favorite treats, those scrumptious dried codfish skins.

One day I was an author and a happy Young Dog. I loved my walks with Gig and my friends. Then, all of a sudden, I couldn't chew or drink water without splashing it all over the floor. I lost my balance and could hardly walk.

And the worst part? I spent three nights in the ICU of an animal hospital without Gig by my side. I was poked and prodded; they took my blood and photos of my insides and stuck me with many needles. I was very scared.

Welcome Home, Pippi!

I'm home now! My little stuffed-animal friends gathered around the big "Welcome Home, Pippi!" sign and clapped when I came into the living room.

Well, it's not a living room anymore. Gig converted it into a hospital clinic because I can't go up and down stairs for a while. Her blow-up bed is right next to my traveling crate, along with a nurse's station with all my meds, an entertainment corner, and an office for Gig. It is very cozy!

Just as I was dozing off, Gig came over to pet me. She told me that the doctors don't know what caused my illness and I needed to be brave. It was going to take a long time for me to get better. She said it was important to find something good in every experience. Frankly, it is hard to find anything good this time, but I have actually thought of some things.

The best good thing, of course, is my new diet. No more dry kibble for me—it's meatballs! Every meal, meatballs hand-fed by Gig. They are so good. I wish you could try them.

Well, I have to say it. Maybe the very best thing is having Gig right here with me all the time, taking care of me, and my stuffed-animal gang welcoming me home!

I hope that if you have ever been sick, you have had someone right by your side.

Bear Gets the Boot

My pen pal, who lives in Atlanta, sent me Bear, a very big stuffed teddy bear. That night Gig put him in my canvas crate among my little friends—Lobster, who is missing a claw; Dinosaur, whose insides are gone ; Flying Squirrel, whose neck hangs on by a thread; and Little Teddy, whose leg fell off.

Bear didn't fit in at all. He has both eyes and his nose; he is not missing any of his limbs; and his insides are intact. There's no way around it: He is a stud, and a preppy one at that, with his bright-red wool scarf, knotted just so.

The next morning, Bear was face down outside my crate. Who knows what happened? I might have been restless in my sleep, given how sick I was, and just booted him out of the crate. Or my little friends may have ganged up on him during the night and shoved him out. Either way, there he was on his face, and none of us even turned him over. He stayed that way until Gig picked him up and tried to smooth his hurt feelings.

Gig sat us all down that morning. She was unhappy that Bear had not been welcomed by my little friends and me. Nothing was said about how Bear must have felt.

Gig asked each of us to think about what happened and what we might do to make Bear feel a part of our little group. I can tell you that there was very little enthusiasm for that: Each of us had our own issues—I was sick and the others were missing body parts. But she said none of that really mattered. Our job was to welcome Bear into our household. So we did!

Bear was given the place of honor. He now leans into the crate and our heads touch and we snuggle. He is a very sweet bear.

39

Stuffed-Animal Clinic

Poor Bear suffered another insult. Gig thought he and my little friends would like to visit Kathy Mac, my illustrator, who offered to do their portraits. (She has done mine so many times that, honestly, I am a bit tired of it all.) Clara, her Airedale, whom I am supposed to mentor, came up to us and—just like that—bit off Bear's nose. It was shameful, really, but maybe Clara did Bear a favor. Now he was maimed like all the rest of my little friends, and no longer Stud Bear.

Kathy, who is clever in all ways, decided some basic work needed to be done on my menagerie. She set up the KMAC Stuffed-Animal Clinic, where she provided services. She stuffed and closed up the gaping hole in Dinosaur's stomach; she stitched Flying Squirrel's head back on; and she provided a prosthetic for Little Teddy and a claw for Lobster.

Kathy supervised a nose job for Bear. It's now a bit off-center. As cute as it is, Bear can no longer breathe out of his new nose. Fortunately, Clara did not mangle his mouth, so he can manage.

My friends are mending from their surgeries and I am recovering from my illness. We will rely on one another for support as we all get better.

We went home a happy gang.

41

Milking It

Do you know the expression "Milking it for all it's worth?" That's what I have been doing for months. I used my illness to my advantage, and now there's no milk left. My privileges are disappearing, and every so often now I hear the words "bad dog."

It really is unfair. I admit, my judgment was flawed the other day, but I think Gig should remember that my illness may have affected it. And perhaps she should even be congratulating me for the recovery I have made from my illness this winter.

The other morning, Gig opened a jar and spread some of the contents on a piece of toast. It was an unfamiliar smell to me, but definitely worth exploring. It is still quite difficult for me to get up on my two hind legs, but I did, and I rested my two front paws on the countertop. With extraordinary effort, I was able to swat the jar off the counter onto a rug, cushioning its fall. Then I nudged it across the rug and managed to push it onto my comfy dog bed.

Even though my chewing function was still impaired, I was able to hold on to that jar and unscrew the top. And inside? To die for. Almond butter—the crunchiest pieces of almond I have ever had, sitting right in the middle of all that butter fat.

Then, of course, you-know-who walked in and was shocked to see my little snout in the jar, almond butter all over my face, licking up that luscious spread. Back to her old ways, she snatched the jar away from me. I will give you this—she was restrained in what she said. In fact, she said I had done a new trick—unscrewing a top off a jar.

What would you have done—congratulated me for a new trick or said, "That's it, Pippi. You have milked it for all it's worth"? You can guess which one Gig did!

Houdini

I find names very confusing, especially nicknames. For the longest time I thought my nickname was "Bad Dog" or "Bad, Bad Dog." It was only when I grew up a bit that I understood that those were not nicknames but had something to do with my behavior. After the weekend I spent at my boyfriend Moose's house, I thought I might actually have a nickname—not one I would have chosen, though. When it was time for bed, I went down into the mudroom with Moose. It was a bit claustrophobic down there—no windows, no fresh air. Frankly, I didn't like it. I waited until Moose was snoring and then tip-pawed up the stairs, only to discover a kiddie gate!

What were my choices? Either give up and go back downstairs or try to get around or through that gate. I remembered the trick lessons I had learned: one of them was how to open a door, and I used it on the kiddie gate! I found myself in the living room, which had plenty of choices for sleeping. I decided on the sofa, where I curled up and went to sleep.

Early in the morning, I woke to a little pitter-patter down the stairs. I leaped from the sofa to a dog bed, curled up, and closed my eyes just as Moose's owner, Liz, walked in. "Oh," she said. "It's Houdini." I kept my eyes closed and wondered if she had said "Who dunnit" and was accusing me of sleeping on the sofa. No, that was not it. She just kept calling me "Houdini." Was this a new nickname for me?

The same thing happened the next night, except the kiddie gate was more securely in place. Challenged but not defeated, Houdini Pippi did it again! In the morning, down came Liz, who said, "Houdini, how did you do it?"

As soon as I got home, I Googled "Houdini," worried sick that it was to become my new nickname. After reading about him, I figured out that Liz was describing my behavior, not giving me a nickname.

Family Reunions

Have you ever been to a family party where you are supposed to remember everyone? For a Young Dog, it can be overwhelming. I try my hardest but, truthfully, sometimes I wander off and climb up on a comfy sofa or bed for a snooze—after a detour to the kitchen to check out the counters. Unfortunately, that's not always an option.

If it were a reunion of dogs, it would be easy to remember them. You can tell them by their smell and, in the case of my cousin Finley, by his piddle whenever he sees me.

But humans? I have worked out how to remember them. There are those who are friendly and come right over and greet me, and those who sit all day long next to a container of dog treats. It is easy to remember the little ones, because they like to poke me, pull my ears, and try to catch my tail. Then there are the bigger kids, who make me do my two-legged high five and make me fetch balls until I just plop down in exhaustion.

And then there's Grandpa. He is my favorite. His face is partially covered by a big handlebar mustache. He rarely shows his emotions, and he doesn't like confusion and noise. I can't always count on a nice head pat from him, but I can count on something much better. When no one is looking, he slips me some of his dinner under the table.

And the best part? Grandpa's mustache! Some of his dinner usually ends up on that mustache. I hang around him, wait until he bends down, and then run over and give his face a good licking. Yum!

How do you remember your relatives?

Bell Ringing

Yesterday we rang the bell for the Salvation Army, a tradition in our town. Residents, employees, and service group members all take turns ringing the bell. Gig told me exactly what was expected of me. She said we would be like the monkey and the organ grinder, with people stopping by and putting coins and bills in the kettle.

There were several groups that demanded different approaches, she told me. I learned quickly. There were the toddlers whose parents (almost always the mothers) would ask if the children could pet me. That was my cue to stand up and wag my tail and smile, even if the toddler poked me in the eye or pulled my ear. Just stand and smile. Into the kettle, *cha-ching*.

Older children would come over on their own and pet me. Gig would slip them a treat, and they would then give it to me. I had to smile and take it gently. *Cha-ching* again. Some passersby just wanted to chat. For them, I had to perform, mostly with my high five. It was simply exhausting, and actually quite difficult to do attached to a leash. *Cha-ching* again!

Then there was my favorite group: elderly people who came over to smile down at me and say nice things. I knew that once upon a time they had their own dogs, and that I reminded them of their beloved companions. We didn't care at all about the kettle with them. We were just happy to give them a memory of days gone past.

And that was it. Gig was very proud of me.

Happy Holidays!

Love

There's a boulder missing in Dogtown. I've looked all over for it and can't find it. It doesn't exist!

I want Gig to take me back to Dogtown so that I can chisel my own inscription into a boulder. It'll say "LOVE" because of the way I feel about her, my family, all my four- and two-legged friends, and even people who don't know me but who read my book.

Gig says marking up a boulder is not allowed. She says it's the thought that counts.

I hope you agree.

Love, Pippi

Bios

KATHERINE L. BABSON, JR., Author

An avid hiker and lifelong dog owner, "Gig" finds her days full of adventure with her young dog, Pippi, by her side. A retired attorney, and a former selectman and town moderator, Gig has served in Wellesley, Massachusetts, town government for more than 50 years.

Gig received her AB from Vassar College, her MBA from Babson College, her JD from Boston College Law School, and her Honorary Doctor of Law from Babson College.

Pippi's adventures are chronicled on Facebook@KatherineBabson.

KATHERINE K. MACDONALD, Illustrator

Entrepreneur, artist, outdoorswoman, and animal lover. Kathy enjoys illustrating Pippi's mischief through the eyes of the dog.

Kathy attended Green Mountain College and received her BA from Central Connecticut College with a major in English and a minor in art. She received her MBA from Olin Graduate School of Business at Babson College. Her business career spanned both for-profit and not-for-profit organizations.

Now retired, Kathy enjoys landscape painting in oils.

www.ingramcontent.com/pod-product-compliance
Lightning Source LLC
Chambersburg PA
CBHW040817120626

46551CB00004B/580